Bulletin Board Power

Bridges to Lifelong Learning

Karen Hawthorne
and
Jane E. Gibson

Illustrated by Jane E. Gibson

2002
Libraries Unlimited
Teacher Ideas Press
A Division of Greenwood Publishing Group, Inc.
Greenwood Village, Colorado

LIBRARIES UNLIMITED
Teacher Ideas Press
A Division of Greenwood Publishing Group, Inc.
7730 E. Belleview Ave., Suite A200
Greenwood Village, Colorado 80111
1-800-237-6124
www.lu.com

Library of Congress Cataloging-in-Publication Data

Hawthorne, Karen.
    Bulletin board power : bridges to lifelong learning / Karen Hawthorne, Jane E. Gibson ; illustrated by Jane E. Gibson.
        p. cm.
    Includes index.
    ISBN 1-56308-917-3
    1. Bulletin boards in libraries—United States. 2. Reading promotion—United States. I. Gibson, Jane E. II. Title.

Z716.35 .H39 2002
028'.9—dc21
                                        2001050538

contents

Bulletin Boards

Preface

Have you ever seen the excitement in a kindergartner's eyes as you shared the book *Where the Wild Things Are*? Or the tears in a fifth-grade boy's eyes when Old Yeller dies? Have you heard the roar of laughter when you read (for the forty-gazillionth time) *Tales of a Fourth Grade Nothing*? Or, perhaps, you have had an entire room rocking as the whole class repeats and tries to say correctly *one more time*: "Tikki tikki tembo-no sa rembo-chari bari rushi-pip peri pembo"? These emotions seen and experienced by librarians and teachers are what make teaching and librarianship worthwhile careers to pursue. The quest to keep this love of reading and learning alive is a consuming one for teachers and librarians.

Bulletin boards can become bridges that allow these emotions to cross the wide waters of indifference and ignorance to allow the enthusiasm for student reading. When students see eye-catching, colorful boards that spark their interest, they rush to the shelves to find the featured books. Perhaps the board features one of their old book friends or entices them to pursue a new quest for a good book.

The collection of boards featured in this book have been favorites of students and have achieved the goal of motivating students to read.

So, create these boards and begin to bridge the gap between inspiring eager, childhood readers and creating *lifetime* readers. Any way to achieve this lifelong love of the printed word and oral stories is worth the effort. Bulletin boards reach many students who never let you know that they did, but the results are evident when all the books featured on the board are suddenly the ones checked out and requested by students.

So...*go for it!* Keep fresh boards up. See and experience the results. Build bridges to motivate lifelong reading.

Introduction

BEFORE YOU BEGIN

We strongly recommend that you refer to our first book—*Bulletin Boards and 3-D Showcases That Capture Them with Pizzazz* published in 1999 by Teacher Ideas Press/ Libraries Unlimited—for more in-depth information on design principles, tools of design, sources of ideas, and other helpful suggestions. Chapter 3 in that book explains the use of book slings, rubber cement, and special effects.

SLINGS AND BOOK LISTS

A sling is a support used to display books on the bulletin board. It enables you to use real books instead of book jackets. These strips of material, string, ribbon, plastic packing strips, and laminating film make it possible to display the actual books in attractive arrangements without damaging a volume. Cut a strip about one-inch wide from the selected material. Then, cut a strip about five- to ten-inches long, depending upon the size of the book. It is desirable to have approximately two inches extra for each book so that this excess can be stapled to the board. Staple the ends of the strip to the background horizontally or at a slight angle where desired. Either insert the bottom corner of the book behind the strip as far down as possible, or open the book and insert half the pages behind the sling, as if it was a bookmark. Larger volumes might need a wider, stronger material.

Many of these boards are purely motivational. Students in K–5 really notice giant candy canes and bugs or real shoes and kites in the media center. Try to make books and reading fun as well as exciting. For older students, multiple copies of book lists may be stapled to the boards to allow students and faculty to take one for their personal use. A "take one" box can be made by cutting an empty cereal box in half, then covering it with a neutral contact paper. This may be used repeatedly.

RUBBER CEMENT

This versatile adhesive turns any lightweight object into a seemingly suspended item simply by applying a dab of it to the object and pressing it against the inside of a glass showcase door or window. It can also be applied directly to the board's laminated background. Raindrops fall, snowflakes drift, fish swim, stars shine, butterflies flutter, and bugs buzz right before the students' eyes; the cement is invisible. When you take down the board, the cement will peel off easily.

SPECIAL EFFECTS

A cloud background can be created from a package of computer paper with a cloud design printed on it. Tape these sheets together in strips that are the width of the board. Then, laminate these strips. Another source for background special effects is wrapping paper with similar cloud designs and items such as stars, snowflakes, and lightning, which enhance outdoor theme boards and showcases.

Use large rolls of art craft paper to cut pieces in various colors to the width of the board and the showcase background. Then, cut these pieces in half lengthwise and laminate. The strips are now ready to be cut, freehand, into strips of green grass, blue waves, white drifts of snow, or brown hills.

Use small Styrofoam pieces to produce a 3-D effect on the boards and showcases. Save Styrofoam scraps for this purpose. Glue little squares to the backs of letters, stars, leaves, or miniature book covers to give depth to the display. Larger strips of blocks turn a napkin into a tablecloth on a table or make a character stand out from the board. Foam packing can become "popcorn" when put into small sacks or boxes obtained from a concession stand.

Strips of Styrofoam may be purchased or found in packing materials. Using foam board to create props also adds dimension and alleviates the boredom of flat objects. A tip to remember about cutting Styrofoam is to rub a knife on a candle to coat it with wax, then it can slice through the Styrofoam without you having to saw it.

Many of the drawn or constructed paper props can be reused. Save the fireplace, once you have made it, and use it for boards in the coming years. Store it in a drawer in a map case. Likewise, laminate the "grass strips" and many of the props made from patterns for future use.

To create "bubbles" for underwater scenes, carefully cut around individual large and small air cells in bubble wrap used for packing. The wrap comes in clear and green. Save any packing materials that might be used for bulletin boards. Other useful types are thin foam sheets, Styrofoam sheets, and odd-shaped pieces of packing. Look at them with your imagination and you can visualize a bench, a table, books, and icicles.

Create computer-generated titles by using a word-processing program. Select a font, type size, and style. Outline is a good choice, because it can be colored to match the board design. Type the title as large as possible, and then print it. This may now be enlarged to the desired size on a copy machine and cut out. For smaller signs, banners, or book lists, enlarge to fit on 8½"-x-14" paper.

COSTS

Do not buy everything listed as props. This could become expensive. Ask fellow teachers or students if they have some of these items. It is surprising how happy these people will be to help. Also look for items and props at garage sales, dollar stores, and other inexpensive variety stores. If you cannot find the exact item, substitute a similar item. You might even come up with a new title or new ideas for the board. Many of these items become standards used in many boards. Leaves, vines, flowers, and acorns always help spice up an autumn board. Snow, snowflakes, and bare tree limbs always help with winter boards. The list goes on and on. You will be amazed by what you think up when you put your thinking cap on.

USE YOUR STUDENTS

Do not forget to use your students to do original decorating of the patterns that you need to produce for a board. An example of this is the "Dog Tales" bulletin board. Students can easily cut these bone patterns out and write their favorite dog book title on them. They can also decorate them. Their work makes your board special, and the students (and their parents) like to see their work featured on your boards. If you do not have access to a die-cut lettering machine for your titles, let the students use your patterns to trace and cut out these letters for you.

PUTTING IT TOGETHER

Developing the display is the next step in becoming a master of bulletin board and showcase creations. Generally, there are months and holidays for which ideas are easily generated. Other times, it is very difficult to even begin thinking about what to do that month. Historically, back-to-school month seems to be a difficult time to decide what to feature. Students have been having a good time playing, relaxing, or doing summertime activities, so they are not necessarily thinking about getting back to reading and researching. This lack of interest is normal and challenges the bulletin board artist to entice them back into the library. On the one hand, January always seems to be another time that is difficult to decide what to create. These problem months require even more effort to create unusual and innovative displays. On the other hand, autumn seems to be an easy season for generating slogans for theme boards and showcases. Scarecrows, autumn leaves, ornamental corn, and hay bales are quickly assembled to carry out these seasonal ideas. Back up the autumn showcase or bookcase display with bulletin boards and displays throughout the area. Sports themes work well during their respective seasons because you can use posters of sports figures to promote almost any subject.

Another consideration in developing holiday displays is local community preferences and the community's views on the subject of holiday observances in the schools. Most public schools allow holiday displays involving Halloween, Thanksgiving, and some variation of the December holidays: Hanukkah, Christmas, Kwanzaa, and other multicultural celebrations. If local opinion prefers, represent October with a football, softball, or soccer theme instead of Halloween. Santa Claus is generally accepted for the Yule season. In private schools, or where allowed, religious holidays offer opportunities to display wonderful collections of crèches, menorahs, and dreidels borrowed from faculty and staff. Thanksgiving can be depicted historically (pilgrims), mathematically (how many quarter-pound servings from a 21-pound turkey?), or as shown in this book, to emphasize reading ("Gobble Up a Good Book"). Local opinion and preferences often suggest appropriate ways to handle the development of displays.

CLOSING COMMENTS

Hopefully, these helps will answer some of the questions you will ask when you begin using bulletin boards as bridges to lifelong reading. Now, *ready, set, go!*

TITLE: Welcome Back to the Reading Patch

BACKGROUND: Board's top half is light blue cloud paper and the bottom half is either a poster, computer-generated garden scene, or brown craft paper

BORDER: None

LETTERING: Red four-inch cutouts

PROPS: Stuffed toy dolls or pictures of stuffed dolls produced by the opaque projector; books; vine greenery; miniature books or small pictures of books cut from publishers' catalogs; rubber cement; T-pins; cotton ball clouds; green crepe paper; floral wire; pinking shears

INSTRUCTIONS: Staple the background to the board. Staple the title to top third of board. Attach green vine down approximately one-third from the top on the left side, across the top and down one-third on the right side. Pin one stuffed doll on the left side. Pin second doll on the right side. Tape or pin books in their hands. Cut out small books from publishers' catalogs. Use rubber cement to glue these small books to the veggies in the garden or, using the brown craft paper as the "dirt," make lettuces or cabbages with the green crepe paper and floral wire. (Pleat a stack of six-inch-wide crepe paper strips in an accordion fashion, then cut the ends into points. Twist a wire around the center; pull folds out on both sides and up, as if making a gift-wrap bow.) Another option for veggies is to purchase artificial ones from hobby or craft stores.

TITLE: Smarty Pants Read!

BACKGROUND: Yellow

BORDER: Red scalloped

LETTERING: Red four-inch cutouts

PROPS: Doll or toddler jeans or slacks; books; newspaper; tissue paper or plastic bags; pushpins or T-pins; reading list; "take one" box

INSTRUCTIONS: Staple background and border to board. Staple the title (centered) in the top third of the board. Arrange pants around the board, as illustrated. Stuff the legs of the pants with paper or plastic bags and pin into "action poses." Place books, book jackets, or paper books in the pants with tops and titles showing above the waist of the pants. Staple the reading list or "take one" box with lists, as illustrated.

TITLE: Overall, Reading Is Best

BACKGROUND: Red

BORDER: Scalloped blue denim fabric or solid blue

LETTERING: Black or yellow four-inch cutouts

PROPS: Doll or toddler overalls; books; paper or plastic bags for stuffing; slings made from denim strips or bandana-patterned material

INSTRUCTIONS: Staple background to the board. Staple border around the sides. Staple title to the upper-left third. Stuff the overalls and pin them across the board in active positions, as illustrated. Using slings, fasten books around the overalls.

TITLE: Olympic Reading

BACKGROUND: Royal blue

BORDER: Gold or purchase Olympic designs border

LETTERING: Red four-inch cutouts

PROPS: Olympic poster; daily newspaper coverage of events; magazine, newspaper, or Internet articles featuring Olympic athletes; heavy gold, silver, and bronze paper (or corrugated cardboard circles painted gold, silver, and bronze); poster board; red-, white-, and blue-striped ribbon (approximately two yards); pushpins

INSTRUCTIONS: Staple the background to the board. Staple border around the sides. Attach title across the top fourth of the board, putting three paper "medals" between the words. Staple or pin Olympic poster at an angle on the upper-left side. Center a rectangle of poster board, proportioned to the board, underneath the title. Draw lines on the poster board for recording America's Olympic winners and events. Make winner's medals with ribbon and metallic paper. Hang by pushpins from the top portion of the list. Add or change the news coverage daily to entice student interest.

TITLE: Back to Reading Basics

BACKGROUND: Black paper for a chalkboard-like look

BORDER: Purchased ABC border or use none

LETTERING: Paint or use colored tape letters on the "blocks" or use rubber cement to glue cutout letters to the blocks

PROPS: Four-inch, square (or larger, depending on the board's size) Styrofoam or cardboard blocks or square boxes of the same size; yellow poster board; spray paint or contact paper to cover boxes; colored tape or paint; black marker; doll; artificial apples

INSTRUCTIONS: Staple the background to the board. Cover boxes or squares with contact paper or spray paint them. Once they dry, paint or tape a letter of the title onto the boxes or squares. An edge may be added to the blocks, if desired. Make a large "ruler" with the yellow poster board. Mark inches with a black marker. Staple it to the board's top-left corner. Cut paper towel rolls lengthwise into arced sections and paint for fake book spines, or cover with paint, tape, or marker to add titles to these spines. Pin blocks on the board to form the title. Add apples, books, and doll, as illustrated.

TITLE: Celebrate Back to School with Books!

BACKGROUND: Solid white paper or wrapping paper with a balloon print

BORDER: Purchased balloon border or use none

LETTERING: Red four-inch cutouts

PROPS: Balloons (soft-sculpture fabric, purchased plastic balloons, real inflated balloons, or poster-board balloons); party streamers; string; pins; black marker

INSTRUCTIONS: Staple the background to the board. Staple border around the edges. There are several options for balloons for this board: inflated ones replaced periodically during the time the board is up; purchased plastic ones from a local party store; or soft, sculptured fabric ones. Pin balloons around the board's edges. Center and staple the title on the middle of the board. Tie strings or pin strings made from curling ribbon from each balloon. Let these strings hang off the board. Use scissors to curl the ribbon. Staple party streamers where needed to fill blank spots, as illustrated. If desired, write book titles with their Dewey Decimal numbers on the balloons.

TITLE: Read to Your Gramps and Granny!

BACKGROUND: Wallpaper or wrapping paper that resembles wallpaper found in dens or family rooms

BORDER: None

LETTERING: Four-inch cutouts in a contemporary color for contrast with the background; solid shows up best on a patterned background

PROPS: Banner proclaiming Grandparents Day; pictures of grandparents seated on a sofa reading to children enlarged from clip art, photos, or the above illustration

INSTRUCTIONS: Staple the background to the board. Staple the title in upper third of board. Make cutouts of grandparents and children reading on poster board by using the overhead or opaque projector. Staple the cutout of readers at the bottom. Make a banner saying "Celebrate Grandparents Day in September!" on computer or letter it by hand. Staple the banner at an angle off the left side. Another option is to have students bring pictures of their grandparents reading to them. Place these photos around the board's edges and even on the wall if your request for pictures produces great results.

TITLE: Clean Up Your Reading Skills

BACKGROUND: Wallpaper or khaki-colored solid paper

BORDER: None

LETTERING: Black four-inch cutouts

PROPS: Child-size broom, mop, and plastic dustpan. (If you have a large board, you could use the full-size ones.); T-pins; thumbtacks or pushpins; book list; "take one" box

INSTRUCTIONS: Staple the background to the board. Staple the title across the upper half of the board, as illustrated. Using T-pins, fasten broom and mop to the board through the upper portion of the straw and strings. Hang dustpan by a T-pin through the hole in its handle. Use thumbtacks or pushpins as props to angle the pan, broom handle, and mop handle. Attach a book list or "take one" box featuring alphabet books, phonics, and favorite easy-to-read books.

TITLE: Don't Be "Dragon"! Get on the Reading Wagon!

BACKGROUND: Yellow

BORDER: Orange

LETTERING: White or black three-inch pin-back letters

PROPS: Raffia or Spanish moss; toy dragon or a cardboard one made using the opaque or overhead projector; wagon made from Styrofoam or cardboard or use a child's toy wagon; books; pushpins

INSTRUCTIONS: Staple the background to the board. Staple the dragon to the board in desired position. Cut a box in half, lengthwise, and paint it red. Using pushpins, fasten box under and around the dragon. Cut circles for wheels and paint them black. Tape or pin wheels in place. Cut out a handle for the wagon, then paint it black. Fasten handle to the wagon with tape or pins. Staple raffia or Spanish moss across the bottom of the board. Staple the title to the upper-right quadrant. Use a black marker to draw "smoke" puffs (on the background) coming from the dragon's mouth. Attach a book to the dragon's claws, then add straw and place more books in the wagon, using slings.

TITLE: Funny Farm Reading

BACKGROUND: Light blue for top three-fourths; green burlap or green paper for the bottom one-third

BORDER: None

LETTERING: Pink four-inch cutouts

PROPS: Two flying pigs (make them using the above illustration or patterns 1 and 2 on the opaque or overhead projector); a large red barn (made using the opaque projector); green raffia or grass from Easter baskets; two reading lists

INSTRUCTIONS: Make the flying pigs (with patterns 1 and 2) and the red barn, as illustrated. Cut them out and paint or color them; then laminate. Staple backgrounds to the board. Staple the title at the top. Staple the barn to the board, then staple a pig on top of each side of the barn, as illustrated. Attach two reading lists featuring funny or humorous books. Students will love it when pigs fly high in the library.

TITLE: Fair Time Reading

BACKGROUND: Sky/cloud wrapping paper or solid light blue paper

BORDER: None

LETTERING: Red four-inch punch-out letters

PROPS: Tent made from striped wrapping paper; Ferris wheel made via the opaque or overhead projector; cotton candy; drink cups and straws; toy hot dogs; toy hamburgers; "take one" box

INSTRUCTIONS: Staple the background to the board. Make tent and Ferris wheel using the opaque or overhead projector. Use the above illustration for patterns or use tent pattern 3. We suggest that you use striped fabric or wrapping paper for the tent. Collect paper cups and straws, then staple or pin them to the board in desired places. Make cotton candy by rolling poster board into cone shapes. Use quilt batting to make the fluffy cotton candy tops by hot gluing the batting to the cones. Fluff it out to add to the effect. If colored cotton candy is preferred, use acrylic craft paint to dab the color on the white cotton. Pin toy hamburgers and hot dogs on the board in desired places, as illustrated, or use patterns 4 and 5 to make them. Staple the title on the top right quadrant. Add cotton-batting clouds above the tent and place the Ferris wheel wherever needed to balance the board. Attach a "take one" box or book lists below the title, as shown.

TITLE: You "Art" to Read These Books!

BACKGROUND: Any primary color (red, blue, green, or yellow)

BORDER: None

LETTERING: Purchased red or black cutouts as well as letters enlarged from clip art or made with art materials

PROPS: Old paint brushes; paint tubes; artist biographies; books about art; palette; colored construction paper or tissue paper; poster board; white glue; pushpins; list of art books (if desired)

INSTRUCTIONS: Staple the background to the board. Use "art" font from clip art enlarged with an overhead projector, or use pattern 6 to make the word *ART*, or form the word using paint brushes, pencils, erasers, old tubes of paint, etc., glued to poster-board or construction-paper letters. Staple these in the middle of the board and arrange the rest of the title as illustrated. Hang a palette (old or new) from pushpins in the upper-right quadrant or make a poster-board palette using pattern 29. Cut out strips of colored paper or tissue to make "paint" brush marks and staple to the board along with an old brush. If desired, attach books to the board using slings. Attach a book list of art books to the palette or use a marker to write the Dewey Decimal numbers for art books on the paint or on the palette.

TITLE: Hats Off! To Reading

BACKGROUND: Flag fabric or use red, white, and blue paper

BORDER: None

LETTERING: Red or black four-inch cutouts

PROPS: Hats (military for Veterans Day; baseball caps; or other kinds of hats: straw, cowboy, stocking caps, etc.); staples; pushpins; list of Caldecott winners or military books; "take one" box

INSTRUCTIONS: Staple the background to the board. Staple the title in the middle. Arrange and staple or pin hats around the board, as illustrated. Attach "take one" box or book lists to the lower-right corner.

TITLE: Batty About Books

BACKGROUND: Black

BORDER: Hot pink, red, orange, or white

LETTERING: Printed on bats with a white paint pen

PROPS: Paint pen; 21 black bats (die-cut from construction paper or made from pattern 7); 21 contrasting paper bats (to match the border's color) from pattern 8; larger plastic bat; "Dracula" doll; book about vampires or Halloween; five very small books cutout from book publishers' catalogs; T-pins or pushpins

INSTRUCTIONS: Staple the background to the board. Staple border around the edges. Print the title on the black bats, one letter per bat, with the paint pen. Center black bats on the bats of contrasting paper and staple to the board, as illustrated, to spell out the title. Staple the remaining six bats and contrasting paper around the board. Staple little books on five of the bats and leave one plain. Pin the larger plastic bat to the upper-right corner. Pin the Dracula doll to the upper-left corner. Spread out the cape and have the Dracula doll hold a Dracula or Halloween book. Any doll may be used by making a cape for it and sticking on fake "vampire" teeth.

TITLE: Fright Night Reading

BACKGROUND: Black

BORDER: Leaf border made with artificial autumn leaves

LETTERING: Four-inch computer-generated letters in a frightening font

PROPS: Poster-board doll cutouts or dolls in Halloween costumes; autumn leaves; bat silhouette; moon; brown paper bags filled with Halloween books or small books

INSTRUCTIONS: Staple the black background to the board. Staple leaf border around the edges. Staple the title to the top left. Make a large orange moon with or without a bat silhouette, and attach it to the top right. Use the above illustration to make the kids in costumes or use stuffed dolls with Halloween masks or infant-sized costumes purchased during seasonal sales. Attach these kids to the board. Add the sacks of books at the dolls' feet. Scatter and staple leaves across the bottom, around the characters' feet. Use the leaves to fill in randomly around the moon, title, and characters' heads with leaves.

TITLE: Creature Feature

BACKGROUND: Yellow

BORDER: Orange wire, jack-o'-lantern garland, or orange-scalloped border

LETTERING: Black four-inch cutouts

PROPS: Purchased Halloween character faces or masks (Frankenstein, Dracula, and a Werewolf, for example); four or five plastic spiders; books about the characters and Halloween themes; thumbtacks; one miniature book; book slings

INSTRUCTIONS: Staple the background to the board. Staple the title in a two-line curve across the upper third of the board. Staple character faces or Halloween masks across the lower portion of the board, as shown. Using the slings, fasten the books around the board. Staple or tack the plastic spiders among the faces and books. Staple the miniature book so that it appears that a spider is reading it. Staple the jack-o'-lantern garland around the edges in a random, twisting fashion.

TITLE: Treats or Tricks the Library Has Both!

BACKGROUND: Brown or dark green

BORDER: None

LETTERING: Orange four-inch cutouts

PROPS: Styrofoam candy corn and peanut-butter kisses or poster-board cutouts made from patterns 9 and 31; orange tissue paper; newspaper; autumn leaves (either artificial or paper cutouts using pattern 10; acorns (pattern 11); small scarecrow (purchased or made); small (two-inch) Styrofoam ball; six-inch wooden skewer; book list; straight pins; thumbtacks; books or book jackets; book slings

INSTRUCTIONS: Staple the background to the board. Staple the title across the top. Pin or tack scarecrow to the center. Make a sucker by inserting the skewer into a Styrofoam ball and covering it with orange tissue paper, twisting it to make a sucker wrapper. Tack it into the scarecrow's hand. Staple leaves and acorns across the bottom. Staple a reading list on the scarecrow's left side. Staple book jackets or books (using slings) to the board on the scarecrow's right side. Make a small "fake" book from a book jacket, or copy of a jacket, and staple under the scarecrow's arm. Attach Styrofoam candy corn and peanut-butter kisses around the board, as illustrated.

TITLE: Dig into a Good Book!

BACKGROUND: Orange or yellow

BORDER: None

LETTERING: Purchased four-inch cutouts or die-cuts in black or brown

PROPS: Child's small plastic shovel; books; brown paper piles of dirt; newspapers

INSTRUCTIONS: Staple the background to the board. Staple the title in the top two-thirds of the board. Attach shovel with T-pins and slant it to the left. Attach Newbery and Caldecott books to the board around the shovel and along the bottom by using slings. Create mounds of dirt by using brown paper bags stuffed with newspapers. Squeeze them into mounds and piles. Staple dirt bags to the bottom, as illustrated.

TITLE: Sweater Weather Reading

BACKGROUND: Sky blue

BORDER: Artificial, silk, soft-sculpture, or preserved autumn leaves

LETTERING: Orange four-inch cutouts

PROPS: Large amount of silk, preserved, or artificial autumn leaves; three or four child- or doll-size sweaters; books with "autumn or fall" in the title; thumbtacks; book slings

INSTRUCTIONS: Staple the background to the board. Staple the title (centered) in the upper half of the board as shown. Thumbtack the sweaters (from the inside) to the board. Attach the book, with slings, to each sweater. Then fold and pin the sweater sleeves so that they appear to hold the books. Staple leaves around the edges and randomly around the title and sweaters.

TITLE: Turkey Ticklers

BACKGROUND: Orange

BORDER: Leaf border (purchased) or solid brown

LETTERING: Black three-inch pin-backs or four-inch die-cuts

PROPS: Turkey; folded turkey jokes; autumn leaves

INSTRUCTIONS: Staple the background to the board. Staple border around the edges. Purchase a fabric or stuffed toy turkey or use pattern 33 to make one with the overhead or opaque projector. Center the turkey and staple or pin it to the board. Arc the title around the turkey tail. Attach folded turkey jokes so that the answer is on the inside. Staple or pin the leaves around the turkey's feet and scatter leaves randomly around the jokes and the title. Some sample turkey jokes:

Q: What do you get if you cross a turkey with an octopus?
A: Enough drumsticks for Thanksgiving!
Q: Which side of a turkey has the most feathers?
A: The outside!
Q: Why do turkeys always go "Gobble, gobble"?
A: Because they never learned good table manners!

Most of these jokes are from riddle books and Internet web sites. They are easy to find.

TITLE: Gobble up a Great Read

BACKGROUND: Yellow

BORDER: None

LETTERING: Red four-inch cutouts or die-cuts (upper and lowercase)

PROPS: Purchased or donated cardboard and tissue turkey garland.

INSTRUCTIONS: Staple the background to the board. Staple the title to the upper third of the board. Staple four lengths of turkey garland in overlapping rows to the bottom two-thirds of the bulletin board. If you cannot find turkey garland or just want to make your own turkeys, use pattern 33 to make as many as needed to produce the desired effect. Students might enjoy coloring their "own" turkey to decorate the board. Not shown: A "take one" box of book lists with a Thanksgiving theme may be attached to the bottom of the board or beside the board.

TITLE: Plenty of Good Books

BACKGROUND: Yellow

BORDER: Purchased or die-cut autumn leaves

LETTERING: Red purchased four-inch cutouts or four-inch die-cuts (lowercase letters)

PROPS: Cornucopia-shaped basket or fashion one from brown paper; autumn leaves from a craft store or artificial ones; autumn book titles printed on orange, red, and yellow paper; T-pins; large leaf and acorn cutouts

INSTRUCTIONS: Staple the background to the board. Staple leaf border around the edges. Staple the title on the right half of the board. Use T-pins to attach the cornucopia basket to the left half. Fill the horn with leaves and book titles, allowing them to spill out. Attach these leaves and title strips with staples. Fasten some leaves and titles on the outside of the horn. Staple large leaves and acorns cutout from patterns 10 and 11 to complete the arrangement.

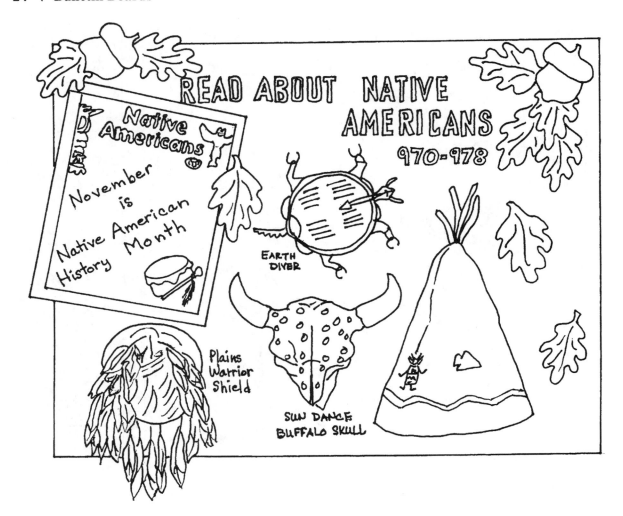

TITLE: Read About Native Americans 970–978

BACKGROUND: Green paper

BORDER: None

LETTERING: White, three-inch pin backs

PROPS: Posters of Native American information; plains warrior shield; Earth diver; sun dance buffalo skull; teepee; dream catcher; leaves and acorns (artificial, real, or from patterns 10 and 11); poster board; brown paper; beige or brown vinyl (optional); markers; small sticks; feathers; newspaper or tissue paper

INSTRUCTIONS: Staple the background to the board. Use pin-back letters and numbers for the title in the top one-third of the board. Using markers and poster board, make a poster announcing Native American History Month. Draw Indian artifacts on brown paper. Color these artifacts with markers and decorate with feathers. Make a teepee from paper or the optional vinyl, fasten loosely on the board, and then stuff paper up into it to make it three-dimensional. Staple the Native American items around the board, as illustrated. Scatter artificial leaves around the board to fill blank spots.

TITLE: Reindeer Riddles

BACKGROUND: Red or white

BORDER: Purchased holly border or other appropriate holiday border

LETTERING: White, red, or green four-inch die-cuts

PROPS: Two stuffed reindeer dolls or opaque projector-generated reindeer; snowflakes (die-cut or purchased); reindeer riddles printed on cards with the answer and source inside; T-pins

INSTRUCTIONS: Staple the background to the board. Staple the border around the edges. Staple the title in irregular ups and downs to the upper third of the board. Use T-pins to secure the reindeer dolls to the board. Pin one to the left side and one to the right side. Staple and arc the riddle cards between the two reindeer. Staple snowflakes around the board to fill in blank spots and add balance. The reindeer riddles card can be produced with computer software that offers colored graphics. These riddles come from joke books and Internet holiday sites:

Q: What reindeer has the cleanest antlers?
A: Comet.
Q: What has six legs, four ears, one tail, two bottoms, four eyes, two noses, and two mouths?
A: Santa Claus on a reindeer.
Q: Where do Santa's reindeer like to stop for lunch?
A: Deery Queen.
Q: Why does the reindeer go over the mountain?
A: Because it can't go under it.

These are just a few examples of the abundant reindeer riddles available through holiday web sites.

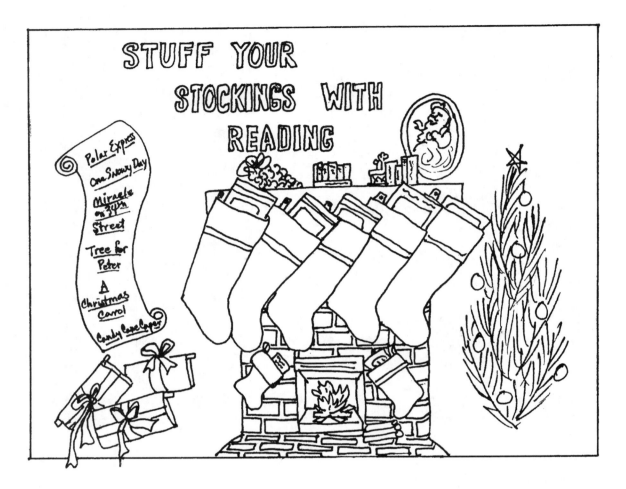

TITLE: Stuff Your Stockings with Reading

BACKGROUND: Green or wallpaper effect wrapping paper

BORDER: None

LETTERING: Red three-inch pin backs

PROPS: Five Christmas stockings; two small stockings; white poster board; red "brick" corrugated paper; twigs; Christmas greenery; pine cone; Christmas ribbon; cutout pictures of books; paperback holiday books; pushpins; pictures of Santa; small light ornaments; scroll of suggested holiday reading

INSTRUCTIONS: Staple the background to the board. Pin title (centered) in the upper fourth of the board. Cut a rectangle from brick paper for the fireplace and hearth (cut a firebox and draw or cut out a "fire" to put in it); staple to the board. Cut a long rectangle from white poster board for the mantel. Staple it at the top of the fireplace. Use pushpins to fasten the larger stockings across the mantel. Tie a ribbon bow on the pine cone and pin it on the mantel top, as if set there. Draw or cut out pictures of books and use them to decorate the mantel. Fasten Santa pictures as "wall hangings." Tape twigs on the hearth. Put seasonal paperbacks into the stockings that you have purchased or produced on an overhead or opaque projector using pattern 32. Hang small stockings low on the fireplace. Use greenery and ornaments to make a Christmas tree. Tie other books with ribbon and staple them to the board (staple the ribbon or slings).

TITLE: Books Light up Our Holidays

BACKGROUND: Red

BORDER: None

LETTERING: Yellow four-inch die-cuts

PROPS: Ten-inch Styrofoam wreath; one-inch-thick Styrofoam sheet; one-inch-thick 10- or 12-inch Styrofoam circle; artificial pine greenery; straw place mat; poster board in a color of your choice; T-pins and straight pins; small "birthday"-size candles in these colors: one black, three green, three red, nine white; three dark blue votive candles; one white votive candle; one or two ears of ornamental corn; brown and yellow or gold craft paint for Styrofoam; books on Advent, Hanukkah, and other world holidays

INSTRUCTIONS: Staple the background to the board. Cut out a Kwanzaa block, called a kinara (pattern 35), from the Styrofoam sheet. Rubbing a knife blade on a candle first makes the cutting easier. Cut out a menorah from the Styrofoam circle by cutting the circle in half, then cut out eight one-inch-wide arcs from the one half. Use four of these arcs and save the other four and the other half circle for something else. Cut a small center section for the "servant" candle as well as a base for the menorah. Use a knife blade to make small holes for the candles in each end of the arcs and in the center section. Make holes in each level of the kinara. Cut out four holes for the votives in the wreath, spacing them evenly around the circle. Cover the wreath with greenery. Paint the kinara brown and the menorah yellow or gold. Using pattern 36, cut out a dreidel from the poster board. Staple the title in the upper half of the board (centered). Attach the menorah on the right, using straight pins, spacing the arcs as shown. Staple the dreidel beside it. Staple the place mat on the left. Attach the kinara on top of it, using T-pins. Attach the corn beside the kinara. Using T-pins, attach the wreath in the center of the board at the bottom. Insert the white votive candle in the top hole and the blue votives in the remaining three holes. Hang the books in the four corners, using slings. Insert the small white candles into the holes in the menorah. Insert the remaining candles in the kinara as follows: green candles on the right, red candles on the left, and the black one in the middle. If the board is away from student traffic, you might consider using a real menorah and kinara block.

TITLE: Ho-Ho-Ho Holiday Classics

BACKGROUND: Green

BORDER: Purchased holly border or other appropriate holiday border

LETTERING: Four-inch die-cuts from red and white candy cane wrapping paper and three-inch white pin-back letters

PROPS: Stuffed Santa head, Santa doll, or Santa cardboard cutout; six-inch red stockings; 12 die-cut candy canes or paper ones made using pattern 12; T-pins; pushpins

INSTRUCTIONS: Staple the background to the board. Staple border to the edges. Attach the Santa head, doll, or cardboard-produced cutout (use pattern 34) to the upper left. Staple the "Ho-Ho-Ho" across the top fourth of the board. Pin the rest of the title under the "Ho-Ho-Ho." Purchase stockings or make them using pattern 32 and the overhead or opaque projector. Scatter the Christmas stockings around the bottom half of the bulletin board. Write holiday titles on the 12 candy cane cutouts or the ones made with pattern 12. Insert these paper candy canes into the stockings and staple them in place.

TITLE: "Cane" 't Celebrate Without Books!

BACKGROUND: Solid red or green paper or solid holiday wrapping paper

BORDER: Purchased candy cane border or a solid coordinating color

LETTERING: Four-inch candy cane paper or die-cut red- and white-striped wrapping paper

PROPS: Three large (36-inch) Styrofoam candy canes or lots of smaller ones, including real candy canes in their wrappers; T-pins; three large green velvet bows

INSTRUCTIONS: Staple the background to the board. Staple border to the edges. Tie a large green velvet bow to each Styrofoam candy cane. Attach two large candy canes with T-pins and pushpins on the left side. One of these should protrude above and off of the board. Attach the third cane on the right side. Staple the title between the canes, as illustrated.

TITLE: The Reading Claus

BACKGROUND: Green

BORDER: Purchased holly or another holiday-themed border

LETTERING: White four-inch die-cuts

PROPS: Large Santa Claus figure—either from this book (pattern 34) or any card, book, or drawing you choose to enlarge using an overhead projector; cotton balls or batting; poster board and construction paper; glue

INSTRUCTIONS: Staple the background to the board. Staple border around the edges. Staple the title to the upper-right quadrant. Use cotton balls or batting to make Santa's beard and fur trim. Make a large "book" from poster board for Santa to hold. Cut around his hands and slip the book into them. Staple Santa on the left side. Staple holiday reading list below the title.

TITLE: Frosty Fiction

BACKGROUND: Dark blue two-thirds down the board and white on the remaining one-third

BORDER: Purchased icicle border

LETTERING: Four-inch aluminum foil die-cuts

PROPS: Two stuffed snowmen dolls or cardboard cutouts; toy sled; books; snowflakes; T-pins; pushpins; book slings

INSTRUCTIONS: Staple the blue background to the board, then staple the white to the bottom. Staple the frosty or icicle border across the top edge. Use T-pins and pushpins to attach one snowman doll to the lower left. Attach the toy sled on the lower right. Pin the second snowman doll on top of the sled to give the appearance that the snowman is riding the sled. Pin or tape books in the snowmen's hands. Randomly staple snowflakes around the board to fill in blank spots. Use slings to attach other books about winter and snow.

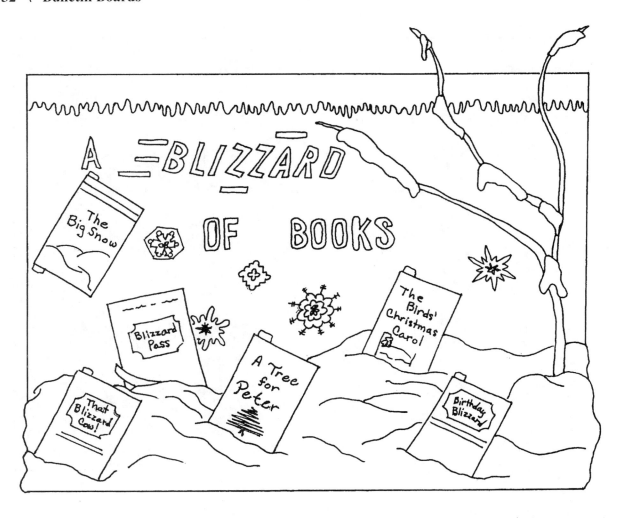

TITLE: A Blizzard of Books

BACKGROUND: Two-thirds from the top is blue, and the bottom one-third is white cotton batting to look like snowdrifts

BORDER: Icicle border at the top only

LETTERING: Three-inch pin backs plus five lowercase "l" letters for dashes

PROPS: Books or book jackets; book list; purchased large tree or a tree limb from your yard; snowflakes; white cotton batting

INSTRUCTIONS: Staple the blue background to the board, then staple cotton batting for snowdrifts across the lower part of the board. Attach the title (centered) across the top third of the board using white pin-back letters. Place books or pictures of books in the snow and on the board. Attach books with slings or staple pictures to the board. Staple a large tree on the right side, extending it off the board. A large limb from the yard could be used for the tree. Drape cotton batting on the tree limbs to create the illusion of snow on the tree. Scatter and staple snowflakes to the entire board to add balance and interest. Attach a wintertime book list on the top right, near the title, if desired.

TITLE: "Knightly" Readings

BACKGROUND: Hunter green or wrapping paper that looks like wallpaper for a den

BORDER: Gold

LETTERING: Gold or black four-inch cutouts

PROPS: Two metal knights or opaque-produced cardboard knight cutouts using pattern 13; a shield (pattern 14); other knight memorabilia, as desired; books; slings; T-pins and pushpins; book lists about knights, fairy tales, and armor, if desired

INSTRUCTIONS: Staple the background to the board. Staple border to the edges. Staple the title across the top fourth of the bulletin board. Center the shield under the title and pin or staple it to the board. Purchase knights or make them using pattern 13 and the overhead or opaque projector. Pin one of the knights on the left side and the other on the right side. Use slings to attach books around the board, as needed. If using one, staple a reading list of books with knights, princesses, fairy tales, and dragons as their theme.

TITLE: "Hi*bear*nate" with Books

BACKGROUND: Orange

BORDER: None

LETTERING: Red four-inch die-cuts; *BEAR* letters in black

PROPS: Upholstery fabric; brass thumbtacks; stuffed bear; small stuffed animal with closed eyes; red brick-patterned corrugated paper; tri-fold picture frame; white poster board; books; book slings; miniature book; twigs; oval place mat; red and black construction paper; book-patterned wrapping paper or wallpaper; tape; T-pins; small doll quilt

INSTRUCTIONS: Staple the background to the board. Staple the title in the upper third, offsetting the letters *BEAR*, as shown. Staple paper "bookshelves" across the lower portion of the board, leaving a "floor" below it. Cut out a fireplace from the brick paper. Make a mantel and hearth from poster board. Make flames from red construction paper and glue on the black background. Tape twigs for firewood and pin them in the fireplace. Fasten frame to mantel with T-pins. Staple place mat in front of the hearth like a rug. Pin sleeping animal on the mat, resting on the miniature book. Cut a chair shape from the upholstery and pin onto the board using the thumbtacks in a chair trim design. Pin bear on the chair with the quilt across its lap and fasten a book in her lap. Use slings to attach books around the title.

TITLE: Let It Snow…Let It Snow I'm Reading

BACKGROUND: Navy blue solid for the top half; cotton batting for large snowdrifts on the lower half

BORDER: None

LETTERING: White three-inch pin backs

PROPS: Snowman doll or opaque projector-produced cardboard snowman cutout; snowflakes; books; T-pins; pushpins

INSTRUCTIONS: Staple the blue background to the top half. Staple and mound up the cotton batting on the bottom half. Use T-pins and pushpins to attach the snowman doll in the center. Cover his bottom half with the cotton batting snow so that it looks like he is part of the snowdrift. Tape or pin a winter book in his hands. Attach the title around the snowman, as illustrated. Attach books with slings randomly over the bottom half, making them appear to protrude from the snow. Staple and scatter snowflakes over the blue background, as needed.

TITLE: Icy Reading

BACKGROUND: Silver wrapping paper or aluminum foil

BORDER: None

LETTERING: Black four-inch cutouts

PROPS: Styrofoam white icicles; books with *ice* or *icy* in the title; snowflakes; copies of the synopsis of each book; spray snow

INSTRUCTIONS: Staple the background to the board. Make enough Styrofoam icicles to hang across the top by using a knife and cutting jagged triangles, as illustrated. The size of the icicles ranges from five inches to 16 inches. Use T-pins to attach the icicles at the top. Spray snow on the upper part of the letters. Staple the title in the middle of the board. Make a copy of the synopsis of each book from its jacket. Use slings to attach books, then staple their synopses by them. Scatter snowflakes all over the board where needed to balance the board and add eye appeal.

TITLE: Dog Tales

BACKGROUND: Blue/cloud paper on the top two-thirds and green grass strips on the bottom one-third

BORDER: None

LETTERING: Black four-inch cutouts or die-cuts

PROPS: Three stuffed toy dogs or three poster-board dogs made using the opaque or overhead projector; dog face, purchased or made using the opaque or overhead projector and pattern 15; twelve dog bones made from white poster board or plain white copy paper using pattern 16; T-pins and pushpins

INSTRUCTIONS: Staple blue/cloud paper to top two-thirds. Staple green paper to the bottom one-third. Make a grass cutout, as illustrated, and staple it at the top of the green paper. Pin the stuffed dogs or cutouts at the bottom, among the grass. Staple the title to the upper fourth of the bulletin board. Staple a cute dog face after the title. Place open books about dogs on the dogs' backs. Have the book titles showing. Make dog bones using pattern 16 or the above illustration. Write the titles of other easy-to-read books about dogs on the bones and staple them randomly around the board, as illustrated.

TITLE: Love Your Books

BACKGROUND: White

BORDER: Purchased valentine border

LETTERING: Red or pink four-inch cutouts

PROPS: Large doll; valentines of various sizes and colors (red, pink, red foil, etc.)

INSTRUCTIONS: Staple the background to the board. Staple the border to the edges. Attach a large stuffed doll or a poster-board doll created on the overhead or opaque projector. Attach a book to the doll's body, then make it look like the doll hugs the book, if possible. Staple the word *LOVE* to the doll's left, and tape the word *BOOKS* to the doll's book or at the middle of its body. Staple *YOUR* to the doll's right, as illustrated. Purchase valentines or make them using pattern 17 and the overhead or opaque projector. Scatter valentines around the board, as illustrated. Write book titles about love or Valentine's Day on the valentines.

TITLE: Dinosaur Lovers Read the 568s

BACKGROUND: Red

BORDER: None

LETTERING: Black four-inch die-cuts

PROPS: Assorted green artificial leaves and fronds; raffia; Spanish moss; dinosaur poster (purchased, drawn, or made with an opaque or overhead projector)

INSTRUCTIONS: Staple the background to the board. Staple the title (centered) down the middle portion of the board as shown. Cut sections of raffia for grass and staple across the bottom. Staple the moss across the bottom of the grass, letting it hang off the board. Cut the dinosaur in half, then staple or tape the halves of the dinosaur so that it appears as if it is behind the board and looking out. Staple leaves around the sides and across the top. Hang Spanish moss on the leaves.

TITLE: Pampered Paws

BACKGROUND: Purple

BORDER: None

LETTERING: White four-inch die-cuts

PROPS: Colored construction paper; markers; photos of students' and teachers' pets; rubber cement

INSTRUCTIONS: Staple the background to the board. Staple the title to the board on an angle at the upper left. Using pattern 18, trace or copy paw prints onto colored paper and cut out. Write book titles from pet-themed books onto paws, then staple them to the board. Have students bring photos of their pets and rubber cement them on paws, then staple them to the board. Be sure to only use the rubber cement on the back of the photo, not both surfaces, so that you can peel off the photos and return them.

TITLE: Hop into Reading

BACKGROUND: Blue

BORDER: "Grass" or grass strip along the bottom

LETTERING: Yellow four-inch die-cuts

PROPS: Grass strip cut from green paper and laminated for future use on other boards; five or six plastic grasshoppers of assorted sizes; books on insects or grasshoppers or books with "hop" or "jump" in their titles; T-pins; fishing line

INSTRUCTIONS: Staple the background to the board. Staple the grass strip across the bottom. Staple the title across the top half, as illustrated. Attach books across the bottom half with slings. Attach one book in the upper-right corner. Tie fishing line around a grasshopper and anchor it to T-pins stuck in the board. Repeat with the remaining grasshoppers.

TITLE: "Toadally" Awesome Books

BACKGROUND: Blue or a patterned wrapping paper with a toad or frog theme

BORDER: Green, purchased

LETTERING: Black four-inch die-cuts

PROPS: Green construction paper; fake frog or toad; white poster board; list of books about nature, animals, reptiles, and amphibians; T-pins; black marker; lily pad

INSTRUCTIONS: Staple the background to the board. Staple border around the edges. Staple the title in the upper left. Staple book list under the title. Cut out a lily pad from the green paper, then staple it to the lower-right quadrant. Fasten the frog with T-pins. Make a cartoon balloon for the frog saying "Read it! Read it! Read it!" or print the words from the computer, cut it out, and then staple it above the frog. Cut a four-by-10-inch piece of poster board and use a marker to write the definitions of a frog and a toad. Staple to the upper-right corner.

TITLE: "Wooden Shoe" Like to Read New Books?

BACKGROUND: Cloudy blue sky and green burlap for grass

BORDER: None

LETTERING: Red four-inch cutouts or die-cuts

PROPS: Two wooden shoes made from poster board using the opaque or overhead projector and pattern 19; purchased silk tulips; T-pins; pushpins

INSTRUCTIONS: Staple the background to the board. Staple the title in the upper two-thirds of the board, as illustrated. Use pattern 19 or the above illustration on the opaque or overhead projector to make the wooden shoes. Staple or use T-pins to attach the two wooden shoes. Staple or use T-pins or pushpins to put three or more silk tulips in each shoe. Write book titles on the tulips or staple the title strips of paper to the tulips.

TITLE: Quit "Lion" Around and Read!

BACKGROUND: Cloudy blue paper

BORDER: None

LETTERING: Black four-inch die-cuts

PROPS: Lion made on the overhead projector or a stuffed toy lion; raffia; fake fur for lion's coat; reading list of books about lions; Spanish moss; artificial plant leaves; T-pins

INSTRUCTIONS: Staple the background to the board. Staple the title across the upper third of the board. Staple raffia and Spanish moss across the bottom of the board. Staple plant leaves around the sides and across the top to give a "jungle" effect. Attach the lion to the lower left. Staple book list to the right of the lion.

TITLE: Soar into Springtime Reading

BACKGROUND: Sky blue

BORDER: Purchased kite or hot air balloon border

LETTERING: Black marker title written on the biggest kite

PROPS: Kites of various sizes with tails (one larger than the others): the larger kite can be a purchased plastic one and the smaller ones can be kite shapes cut from book-patterned wrapping paper (using pattern 20) with tails made from ribbons; broad-tip marker; ribbons

INSTRUCTIONS: Staple the background and border to the board. Write the title on the large kite with a broad black marker. Fasten large kite in the middle, arranging the tail and stapling it to the board, as illustrated. Staple the smaller kites around the board, letting their tails hang down off the board.

TITLE: Books Are Real "Quack" Ups

BACKGROUND: Sky blue for the upper two-thirds; grass strip cutout for the bottom one-third

BORDER: None

LETTERING: Black four-inch die-cuts

PROPS: Two white stuffed ducks or two ducks made from poster board using pattern 21 and an opaque or overhead projector; T-pins and pushpins; book list of joke books and humorous books

INSTRUCTIONS: Staple the blue background to the board. Staple the grass strip cutout across the bottom. Staple the title to the upper third of the board, as illustrated. Use T-pins and pushpins to attach the stuffed ducks or staple the poster-board ducks to the board. Place the ducks on opposite sides, facing each other. Staple the book list between them.

TITLE: Spring Fever???? Perfect Cure = Rx Reading

BACKGROUND: Green

BORDER: Artificial flowers

LETTERING: Computer-generated and enlarged

PROPS: Artificial flowers; poster board; red and black markers; yellow paper or marker

INSTRUCTIONS: Staple the background to the board. Staple artificial flowers around the upper-left corner and across most of the top, as illustrated. Using a copier or overhead projector, enlarge the computer-generated title on yellow paper or color it yellow and staple it across the top and bottom. On poster board, draw an arm and hand holding a thermometer or enlarge pattern 22. Cut it out, then cut around the outlines of the end of the thumb—so that the hand can "hold" the thermometer—and staple it to the board. Use the red marker to draw in the "temperature reading" on the thermometer. Draw a prescription bottle on poster board with the black marker or use pattern 23, making a label as shown. Cut out the pill bottle and staple it to the right side of the board.

TITLE: Recipe for Good Reading

BACKGROUND: Yellow

BORDER: None

LETTERING: Red four-inch die-cuts

PROPS: Wire whisk; wooden spoon; fishing line; T-pins or pushpins; empty egg carton; empty flour sack; chef's hat or white paper sack; chef's apron; white poster board; black marker

INSTRUCTIONS: Staple the background to the board. Staple the title across the upper third. Hang the apron from the upper-right corner, using a pushpin to secure it. Draw an open book on the poster board and write the "recipe," as illustrated. Center this "book" on the board and staple it. Tie fishing line around the whisk and wooden spoon, then use it to anchor the utensils onto the board with T-pins or pushpins. Pin a chef's hat onto the board or make one from a white sack. Pin the egg carton below the hat. Make "eggs" from poster board or use purchased ones from craft stores. Pin the flour sack below the utensils. Label all of these with the marker or make a labeling strip of poster board and attach.

TITLE: Fish Tales

BACKGROUND: Blue or fish-patterned wrapping paper

BORDER: None

LETTERING: Red or white four-inch die-cuts

PROPS: Four stuffed cloth fish or purchased cardboard cutouts, or use pattern 24 to make them, then color them; "bubbles" cut from bubble wrap; reading list of fish-themed books; T-pins; rubber cement

INSTRUCTIONS: Staple the background and border to the board. Staple the title (centered) across the top. Center the reading list below the title. Attach the fish around the list with T-pins. Use rubber cement to affix the bubbles to the background above the fishes' mouths.

TITLE: Buggy About Books

BACKGROUND: Green

BORDER: None

LETTERING: Orange four-inch die-cuts

PROPS: Plastic bugs; clip art "bug" alphabet or plastic fishing worms; poster board; markers; T-pins; fishing line or rubber bands

INSTRUCTIONS: Staple the background to the board. Enlarge clip art "bug" Os and Gs, or make your own, then color and cut them out to complete the title. You might also use plastic fishing worms purchased from a sporting goods store to make these letters. Staple the title across the upper two-thirds of the board. Attach the bugs to the board, as illustrated.

TITLE: Showers of Books

BACKGROUND: Navy blue or dark blue

BORDER: None

LETTERING: Four-inch aluminum foil die-cuts

PROPS: Umbrella; small aluminum foil raindrop cutouts; large aluminum foil raindrops; books about weather or with "April" in the title; T-pins and pushpins; slings

INSTRUCTIONS: Staple the background to the board. Attach a large partially opened umbrella in the upper left. Staple the title next to the umbrella. Create raindrops from aluminum foil. Hang books on the large aluminum foil raindrops using slings, as illustrated. Staple small and large raindrops around the board.

TITLE: Follow the Yellow Brick Road to Reading

BACKGROUND: Sky blue for the top half; yellow brick road made from yellow vinyl for the middle and green grass paper or burlap on either side of the yellow brick road

BORDER: None

LETTERING: Black three-inch pin backs

PROPS: Six purchased *Wizard of Oz* dolls or use costumes for any 11½-inch dolls; yellow vinyl to cut out a yellow brick road; wrapping paper tubes, laminating tubes, paper towel tubes, etc.; emerald green spray paint; small poppy flowers to scatter in the green grass; T-pins, pushpins; cotton balls; glue gun; glitter

INSTRUCTIONS: Staple the blue background to the upper half of the board. Make a yellow brick road using the above illustration or by freehand following the rules of perspective. With a black sharpie pen, draw bricks on the yellow vinyl. Attach yellow brick road in the center, extending down to the bottom. Staple green paper or green burlap on either side of the road. Stick or staple small silk poppies throughout the green grass until it looks like a field of poppies. Pin the title (centered) in the top third of the board, as illustrated. Place a witch doll to the left of the title. Hot glue the laminating tubes, or paper towel tubes of varying heights, together, then spray paint them emerald green and sprinkle with glitter. Attach the Emerald City to the upper right. Attach the remaining characters along the yellow brick road and in the grass. Attach small strips of paper with fantasy book titles on them to the Emerald City. Pull cotton balls apart for clouds and glue them to the city and across the blue sky. Make a little sign over the city door reading "Library."

TITLE: Read a Big Hit

BACKGROUND: Baseball wrapping paper or solid brown wrapping paper

BORDER: Red scalloped

LETTERING: Black four-inch die-cuts

PROPS: Baseball bat; six- or eight-inch poster-board cutout circles made using the opaque or overhead projector and pattern 25; T-pins or pushpins; books about baseball; book slings; masking tape

INSTRUCTIONS: Staple the baseball wrapping paper to the board. Staple the red corrugated border to the edges. Attach the baseball bat at an angle using T-pins and pushpins on the right side, as illustrated. Staple the title (centered) in the upper left two-thirds of the bulletin board, as illustrated. Make the baseball cutouts on a projector with pattern 25 or use die-cut-produced circles. Use a red sharpie to make the arced stitches on each white ball. Using slings, hang books around the board. Use doubled masking tape to stick baseball cutouts on the books. Staple the balls around the bat and title, as illustrated.

TITLE: "Reel" Good Reading

BACKGROUND: Red

BORDER: None

LETTERING: Black three-inch pin backs

PROPS: Large reel of movie film; small reel of film; reading list of movie-related books; one or two books with a movie theme or biographies about actors/actresses; pushpins; thumbtacks; T-pins

INSTRUCTIONS: Staple the background to the board. Take several reels of film from your audio/visual room and hang the large reel in the upper-left corner with T-pins. Attach the title next to the reel. Staple the reading list in the middle. Attach books, using slings, or copies of the book covers around the board. Hang the small reel in the lower right. Unwind some of the film and drape it across the board over pushpins. Use a thumbtack to hold the end of the film without piercing the film, as illustrated.

TITLE: Get Hooked on Reading!

BACKGROUND: Blue

BORDER: None

LETTERING: White four-inch pin backs

PROPS: Three wire coat hangers; string; purchased fish "pillows" or ones made from preprinted fabric and stuffed with batting; sheet of white foam packing film; small banner saying: "Dive into the Public Library This Summer"; T-pins; wire cutters and pliers; tape

INSTRUCTIONS: Staple the background to the board. Mount the title across the top in a gentle arc. Using T-pins, fasten the fish in the middle, facing each other. Cut off the hooks of the hangers, plus an inch of hanger. Bend the inch of wire back into a loop. Tie a length of string through each loop to make a fishing line and hook. Use string instead of real fishing line in order to make it a visible part of the board design. Using T-pins, fasten the hooks as shown. Tape the strings to the top, tucking the ends behind the board. Draw waves on the foam packing, then cut it to fit across the board. Cut out the waves and staple them to the board. Staple the banner below the fish and slightly behind the waves.

TITLE: Riddle Me This…Riddle Me That…Do You Know Where Riddle Books Are Kept?

BACKGROUND: Green or black

BORDER: None

LETTERING: Black or white three-inch pin backs

PROPS: Overhead projector and poster board; riddle cards; pin-back question marks; small card with call numbers for sections containing riddle books

INSTRUCTIONS: Staple the background to the board. Using the overhead, copy the above illustration on poster board, then color and cut it out. Staple it on the upper right. Write riddles on folded pieces of paper with the answers inside. Attach the title down the left side. Staple call number card under the illustration. Staple riddle cards across the bottom portion so that students can lift them to see the answers. Attach pin-back question marks around the board.

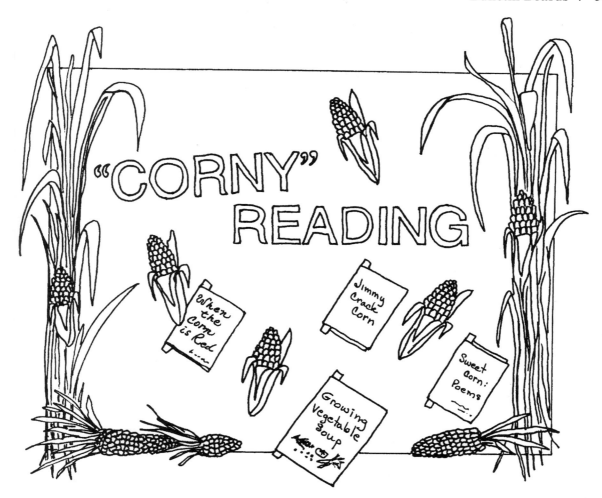

TITLE: "Corny" Reading

BACKGROUND: Orange

BORDER: None

LETTERING: Yellow four-inch die-cuts or computer-generated letters

PROPS: Two cornstalks (dried or made from grasses); three or four ears of ornamental corn; green and yellow construction paper; black marker; book slings; T-pins

INSTRUCTIONS: Staple the background to the board. Staple a cornstalk on each side. Staple the title across the top. Using pattern 26, cut the entire corn shape from green paper. Then, use the yellow to make individual corn "kernels," gluing them in an overlapping pattern to make the "ears." Draw the "husk" lines with the marker. You might also buy artificial corn at a hobby store and pin them into the cornstalks on the board. Staple the corn onto the stalks and around the board between books on corn, farm jokes, or gardening themes. Attach ornamental corn across the bottom with T-pins through the husks and as supports under them. *Suggestion:* Copy the corn pattern and let students color the ears to decorate the board as a border.

TITLE: Fan-tasy Books

BACKGROUND: Aqua

BORDER: None

LETTERING: White four-inch cutouts

PROPS: Large paper folding fan; pushpins; reading list of books with "fan" and "unicorn" in the title; purchase a picture of a unicorn, copy a picture from a book, or use this illustration

INSTRUCTIONS: Staple background, list, and pictures as shown. Pin the fan, opened, with push pins through the open supports.

TITLE: Jog into Reading and Exercise Your Mind

BACKGROUND: Blue

BORDER: None

LETTERING: Red or white four-inch die-cuts

PROPS: Five sweatbands; five running shoes (don't have to match); towel; books with "running" or "jog" in the title; T-pins

INSTRUCTIONS: Staple the background and title to the board. Pin sweatbands across the top. Pin the towel on the right side. Using slings, hang the books around the bottom half of the board. Pin the shoes in active positions among the books.

TITLE: "Eggstra"-ordinary Reading

BACKGROUND: Green

BORDER: Yellow

LETTERING: Yellow four-inch die-cuts

PROPS: Poster board; markers or paint and brushes; reading list of Caldecott winners or books about spring, Easter, bunnies, egg themes

INSTRUCTIONS: Staple the background to the board. Staple the title to the board, arching the "Eggstra" part to emphasize the intended pun. Using enlarged pattern 27, or, drawing freehand, make and cut out giant eggs from the poster board and decorate with paint or markers. Staple in a cluster on the lower left quadrant. Staple the reading list on the lower right. *Variation:* Use glue, glitter, braid trim, sequins, etc., to make the eggs "eggstraordinary."

TITLE: Wrestle in Summer Reading

BACKGROUND: Black

BORDER: None

LETTERING: Red or yellow four-inch die-cuts for *WRESTLE*; red pin backs for the remainder; white pin backs for *WRESTLEMANIA*

PROPS: Wrestling books; overhead projector-produced or wrestling poster; poster board; markers or crayons; rubber cement; book slings

INSTRUCTIONS: Staple the background to the board. Using the overhead projector, enlarge a picture of a wrestler on the poster board. Color and cut it out, or use a purchased wrestling poster. Make a "Reading Champ" buckle for either the drawing or the poster, then rubber cement it on the wrestler. Staple the wrestler on the left side. Staple and attach the title and *WRESTLEMANIA* as illustrated. Hang the books using slings. Hang one book in the wrestler's hands wherever they are in your picture or poster.

TITLE: You "Auto" Read!

BACKGROUND: Wrapping paper with antique cars or racing cars

BORDER: Red corrugated border

LETTERING: Black four-inch cutouts

PROPS: Four computer-generated antique cars using different graphic programs or using pattern 28 to create the cars with the opaque or overhead projector.

INSTRUCTIONS: Staple car-patterned wrapping paper to the board. Staple the border to the edges. Center the title in the middle, as illustrated. Staple two cars on each side, facing each other, as shown.

TITLE: Kool Kats Keep Kool by Reading

BACKGROUND: Blue

BORDER: None

LETTERING: Red or orange four-inch die-cuts

PROPS: Large yellow paper sun; beach towel; paper parasol; two starfish (real or artificial); stuffed cat; sunglasses; books about summer or the seashore; T-pins; book slings; brown paper; pushpins

INSTRUCTIONS: Staple the background to the board. Staple sun in the upper right corner. Staple the title in three rows on the top left quadrant. Cut a "beach" from brown paper or use sandpaper, then staple it across the bottom. Attach cat to the bottom left corner. Hang books on the board and in the cat's paws using slings and pushpins for support. Hang starfish on pins. Put sunglasses on the cat.

TITLE: Race into Reading

BACKGROUND: Black and white checkerboard or white plastic tablecloth

BORDER: Black

LETTERING: Red four-inch punch outs or die-cuts

PROPS: Three or four plastic toy racecars; black road made from laminated construction paper with white lane marks; T-pins; small black and white checkered flag; two racecar books; book slings

INSTRUCTIONS: Staple the background to the board. Staple border around the edges. Staple the title in the upper-left corner. Staple the road to the board. Attach plastic toy cars to the road, using T-pins if necessary. Hang books at the beginning and end of the road. Fasten checkered flag by the finish line, if desired.

TITLE: Everybody's Reading

BACKGROUND: Red

BORDER: Book-design wallpaper border

LETTERING: Black pin backs

PROPS: Bookmarks; posters; magazine illustrations; notepaper; *anything* showing readers (people, pets, stuffed animals, etc.) reading.

INSTRUCTIONS: Staple the background to the board. Staple book border across the bottom. Arrange the reading pictures attractively on the board. Pin title across the top. *Suggestion:* Ask students for pictures of them reading or their family and friends reading. Attach these pictures and even extend them off the board if your request generates lots of pictures.

TITLE: "Purrrfect" Books

BACKGROUND: Purple

BORDER: None

LETTERING: Pink four-inch cutouts or die-cuts

PROPS: Two white stuffed toy cats or two cats created on the overhead or opaque projector; two balls of yarn, any color; reading list of books with a cat theme; paperback book; T-pins

INSTRUCTIONS: Staple the background to the board. Staple the title to the upper center third of the board. Pin cats on the right and left, as shown. Staple reading list between the cats. Pin balls of yarn at the beginning and end of the title. Unroll some yarn and let it hang down by the cats. Staple the yarn so it falls gracefully. Fasten a paperback book in one of the cat's paws.

TITLE: Books Are Your Ticket to Anywhere

BACKGROUND: Black paper

BORDER: Red, or buy rolls of tickets used at sporting events or carnivals and attach them as a border. The border in the above illustration has a two-ticket width.

LETTERING: White pin-back letters or tear off strips of tickets to make letters

PROPS: Tickets; pattern 30 enlarged on the opaque projector, with others torn apart and stapled all over the board; book titles about vacation places; travel brochures or magazines; glue

INSTRUCTIONS: Staple the background to the board. Staple double rows of tickets to all four sides. Staple the title across the top and bottom, with a large ticket in the center. Cut out pictures of exotic destinations and glue them to the large ticket in an overlapping, random arrangement. Write book titles on single tickets and randomly staple them all around the board, as needed, to balance the board.

TITLE: "Cool" Books

BACKGROUND: Blue

BORDER: None

LETTERING: Yellow four-inch die-cuts

PROPS: Three-feet by two-feet piece of clear laminated film; three or four books with "cool" or "lemon-ade" in the titles; poster board; markers; empty gift wrap tubing; white paper; tape; slings; pushpins

INSTRUCTIONS: Staple the background to the board. Staple the title as shown. Staple one short end of the clear laminate to the board about two feet in and about six inches from the left side. This proce-dure is shown with dotted lines on the illustration. This piece of laminate is the back of the glass. The clear laminate will stick out on the left side of the board. Hang the books with slings on top of the laminate, as shown. Curve the other end of the laminate to the right, over the books, bowing out like the front side of the glass, then staple the end of the laminate to match the back right side. This makes a glass with "book" ice cubes. Wrap the tube with white paper to make a straw and put it into the glass, anchoring it inside the top with a white pushpin. Draw a pair of sunglasses on the poster board, then color and cut it out. Staple it in the lower-right corner. Often large, oversized sunglasses can be found at novelty and "dollar" stores. Using the real thing adds a more 3-D effect if you are able to find this item.

TITLE: Swing into Reading

BACKGROUND: Blue for the upper two-thirds; green artificial turf for the lower one-third or use wrapping paper with golf scenes

BORDER: None

LETTERING: White four-inch die-cuts for *SWING*; white three-inch pin backs for the remainder

PROPS: Child's plastic golf club or a real one; white poster board; black markers; four elementary books about golf; golf cap or sun visor; pushpins; fishing line

INSTRUCTIONS: Staple the background to the board. Staple *SWING* in an inverted arch in the upper-left corner, then pin the rest of the title below it. Pin the golf cap in the upper-right corner. Wrap and tie fishing line around the club handle in two places. Hang on push pins. Cut out a circle of poster board and use the marker to make golf ball "dimples" on it. Staple this ball to the board by the golf club, or use a plastic golf ball and hang it on the board using T-pins.

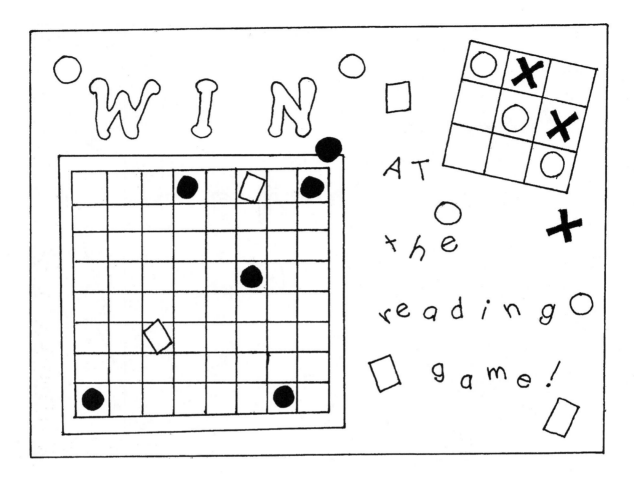

TITLE: Win at the Reading Game!

BACKGROUND: Yellow paper

BORDER: None

LETTERING: Red four-inch cutouts for *WIN*; red three-inch pin backs for the rest

PROPS: Cardboard checkerboard; checkers; tic-tac-toe game board; other game boards, as needed, to fill your bulletin board; small books cut from publishers' catalogs

INSTRUCTIONS: Staple the background to the board. Pin the checkers game board in the lower left corner. Use rubber cement to affix checkers to the game board. Pin the tic-tac-toe game board in the upper right corner. Staple *WIN* above the checkerboard. Use the pin-back letters to finish the title, as illustrated. Rubber cement more checker pieces and small books cut from publishers' catalogs, as illustrated.

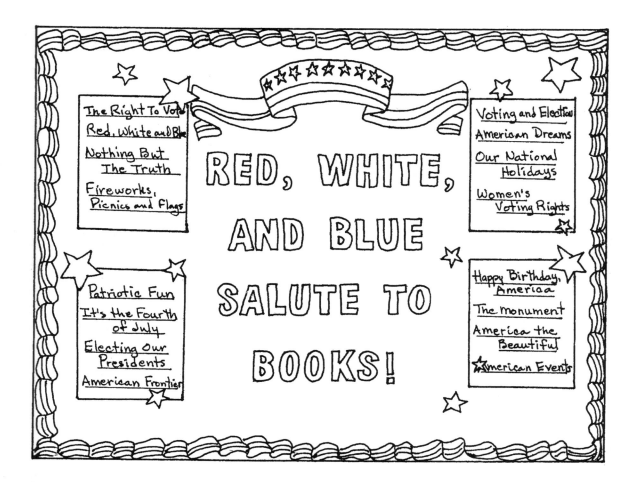

TITLE: Red, White, and Blue Salute to Books!

BACKGROUND: Red

BORDER: Purchase flag pattern or solid blue or red- , white- , and blue-striped border

LETTERING: White three-inch pin backs

PROPS: Stars of various sizes in red, white, blue, and yellow; purchased bunting-type decoration or a wide red, white, and blue ribbon; four reading lists of patriotic themes, such as people, holiday ideas, history, elections, etc., or use the actual books and book slings

INSTRUCTIONS: Staple the background to the board. Staple border around the edges. Pin the title down the middle third of the board, as shown. Attach bunting or drape a ribbon across the top. Staple reading lists or hang books down each side. Staple stars around the board, overlapping the lists.

TITLE: Sparkling Summer Reading

BACKGROUND: Royal blue

BORDER: None

LETTERING: Red four-inch die-cuts for *SPARKLING*; three-inch pin backs for *SUMMER READING*

PROPS: Two thin 18-inch dowel rods; three empty toilet paper rolls; one empty paper towel roll; striped wrapping paper; starry wrapping paper; shredded silver foil gift excelsior; books with "firecracker" or "sparkle" in the title; colored cotton balls; tape; three pipe cleaners

INSTRUCTIONS: Staple the background to the board. Staple *SPARKLING* in an uneven line across the top. Pin the rest below *SPARKLING* to complete the title, as illustrated. Tape or hang the dowel rods from T-pins on each side, and staple shredded foil at the tip to resemble sparklers, or you could use two cheerleader pompons. Cover the paper towel roll with striped paper and tape at an angle across the bottom of one of the "sparklers." Pull three colored cotton balls into larger, fluffier balls and staple so that they look like fireballs coming from a Roman candle. Cover the toilet paper rolls with the starry paper, twisting one end of the paper to cover the open end, and stick a pipe cleaner "fuse" in it. Tape these "firecrackers" on the board, as illustrated. Using slings, hang books across the bottom half of the board.

TITLE: Splash into Summer Reading

BACKGROUND: Blue

BORDER: None

LETTERING: White four-inch die-cuts for *SPLASH*; white three-inch pin backs for the remainder

PROPS: White poster board; inflatable child's swim ring; child's inflatable "floaties"; swim mask; plastic snorkel; reading list of water and/or swimming-related books; tape; T-pins

INSTRUCTIONS: Staple the background to the board. Staple *SPLASH* letters irregularly across the upper-left corner. Pin remainder of the title across the board below it. Cut water "splashes" from poster board and staple around *SPLASH*. Staple reading list in the center of the board below the title. Hang the swim mask from two T-pins in the lower-left corner. Tape the snorkel to the board, at an angle, across the bottom right corner of the list.

Pattern 1

Pattern 2

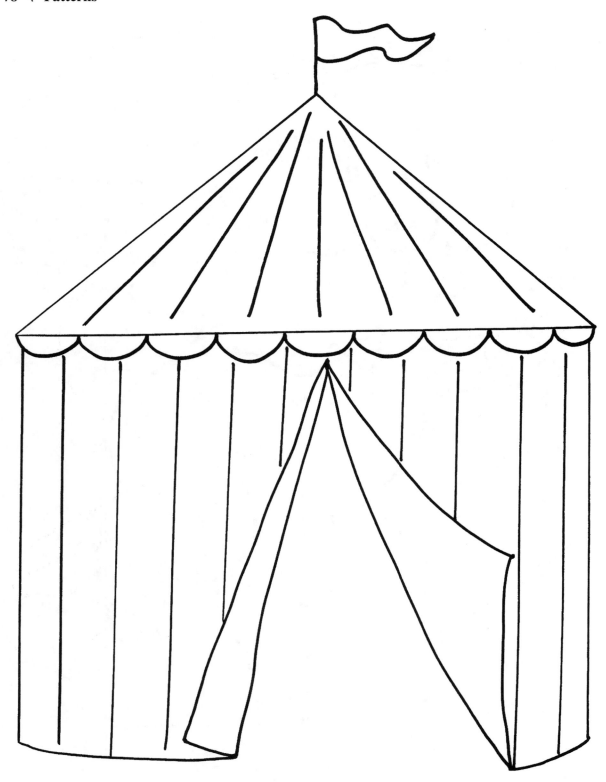

Pattern 3

Pattern 4

Pattern 5

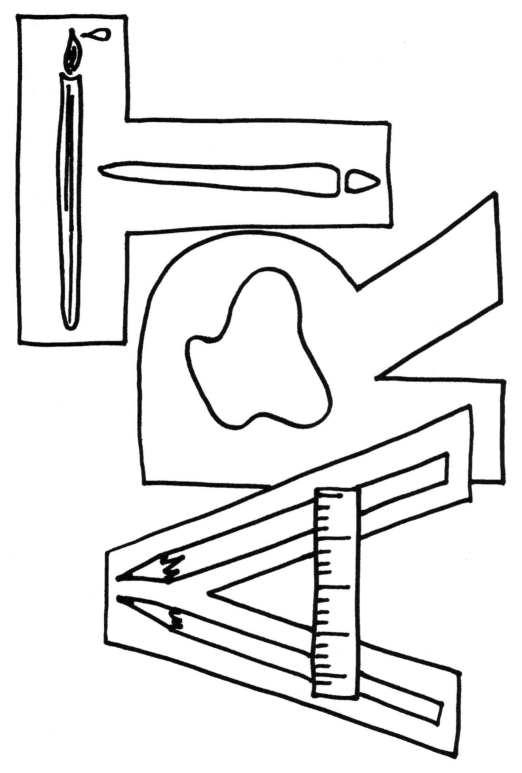

Pattern 6

Pattern 7

Pattern 8

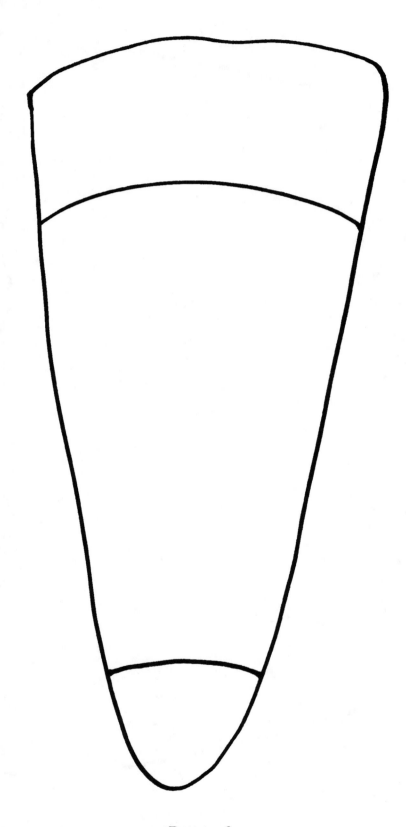

Pattern 9

Pattern 10

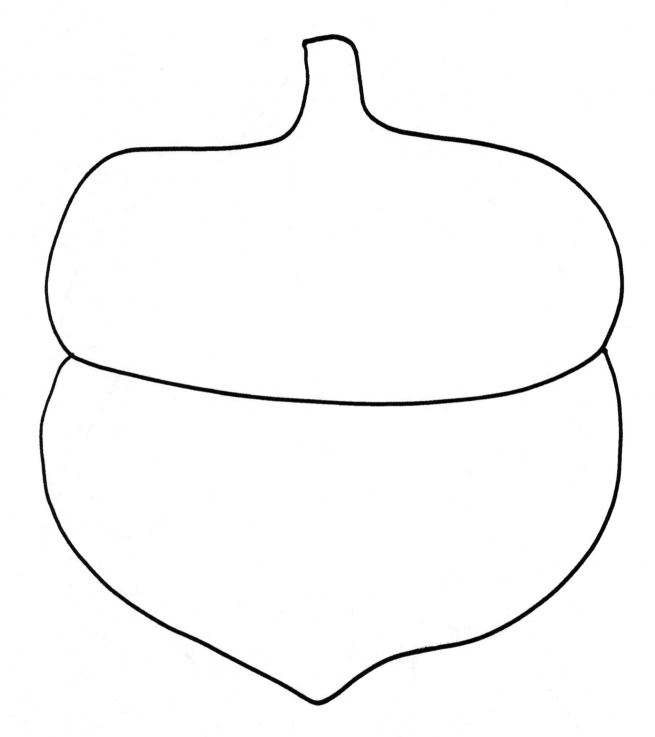

Pattern 11

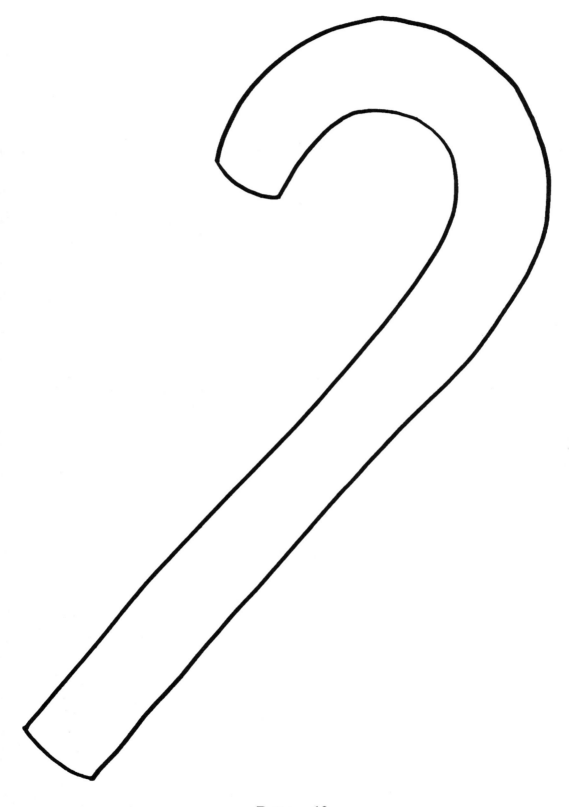

Pattern 12

Pattern 13

Pattern 14

Pattern 15

Pattern 16

Pattern 17

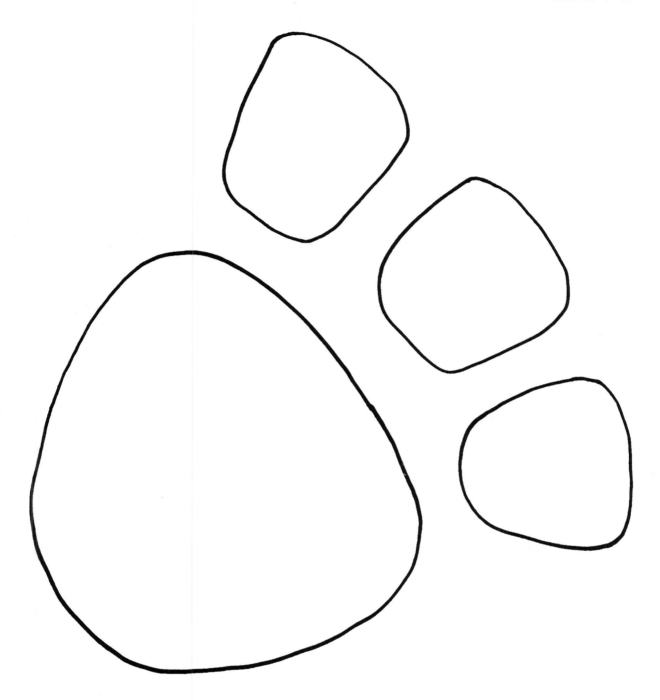

Pattern 18

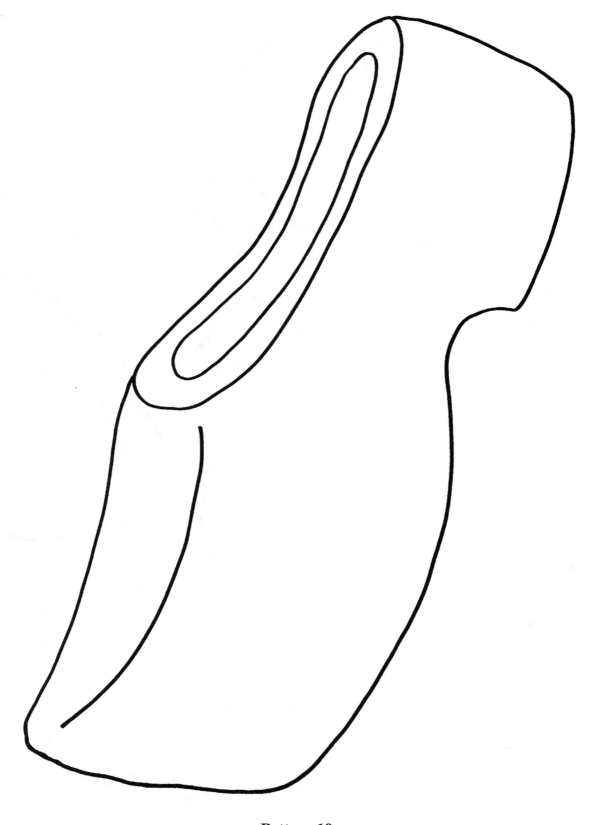

Pattern 19

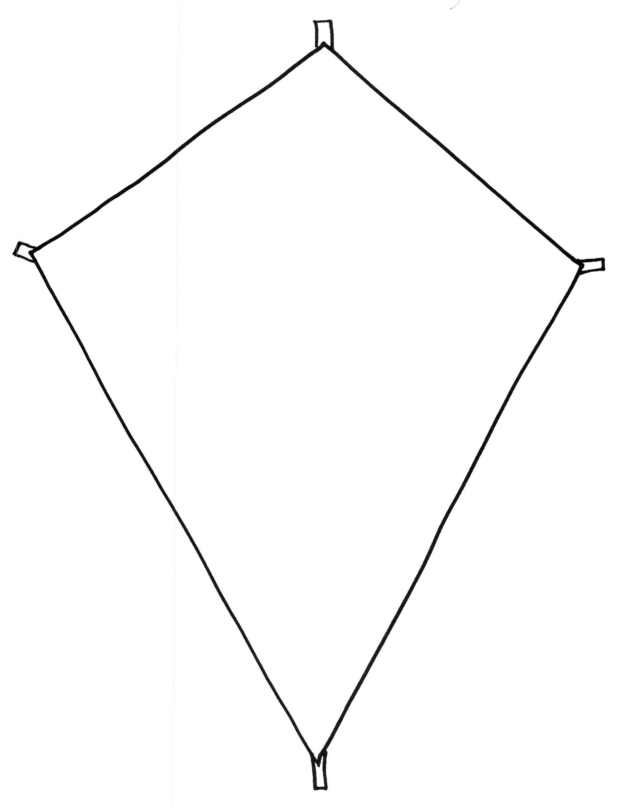

Pattern 20

Pattern 21

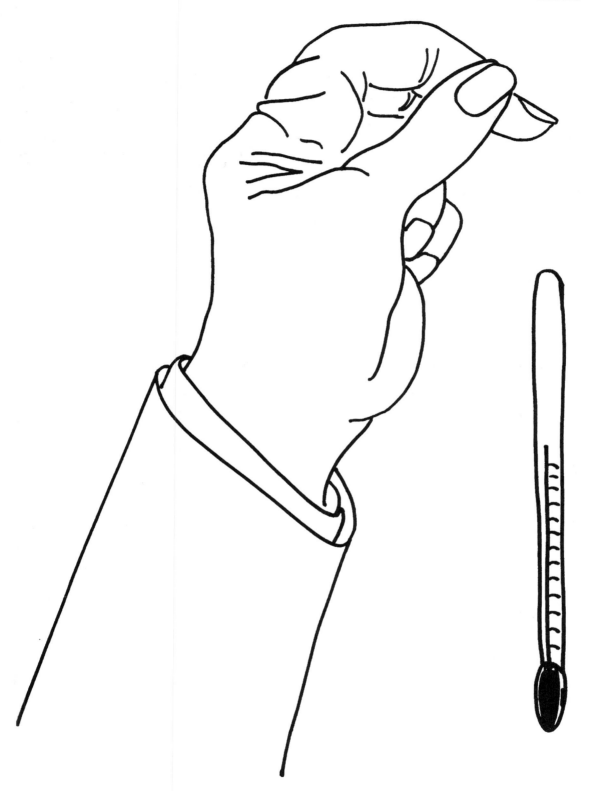

Pattern 22

Pattern 23

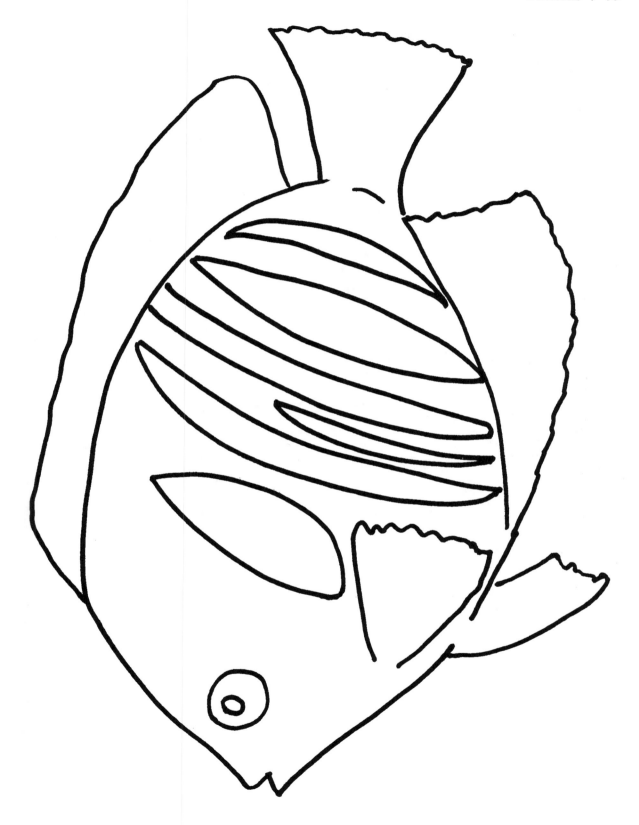

Pattern 24

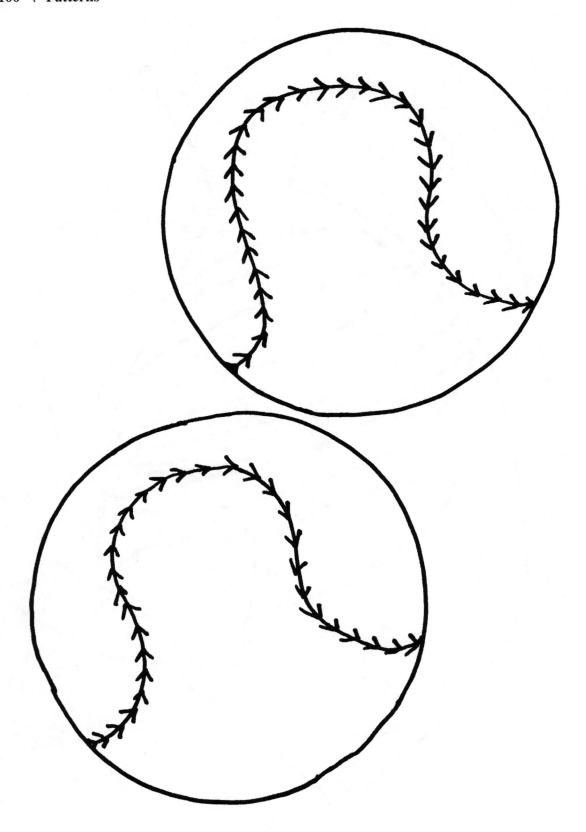

Pattern 25

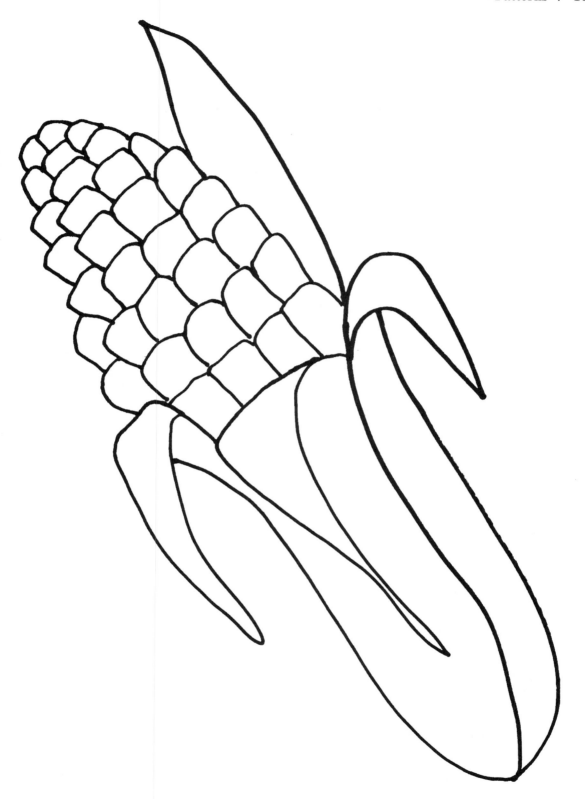

Pattern 26

Pattern 27

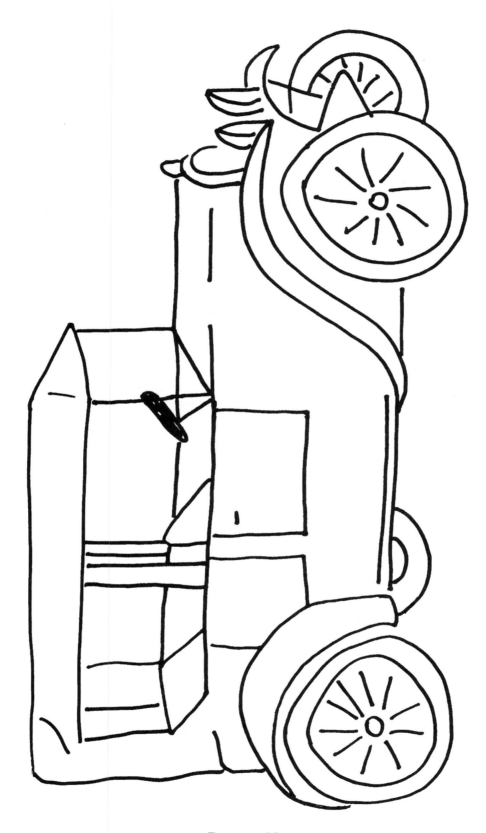

Pattern 28

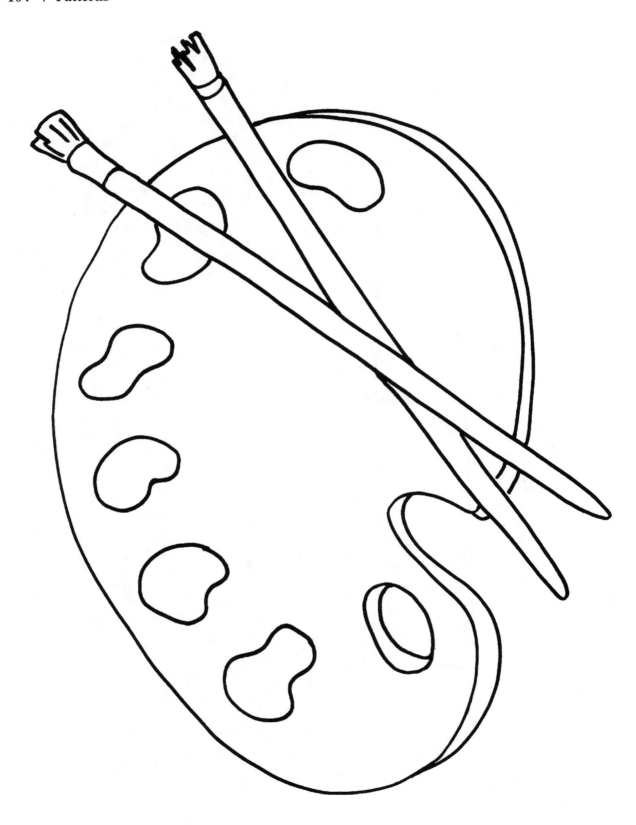

Pattern 29

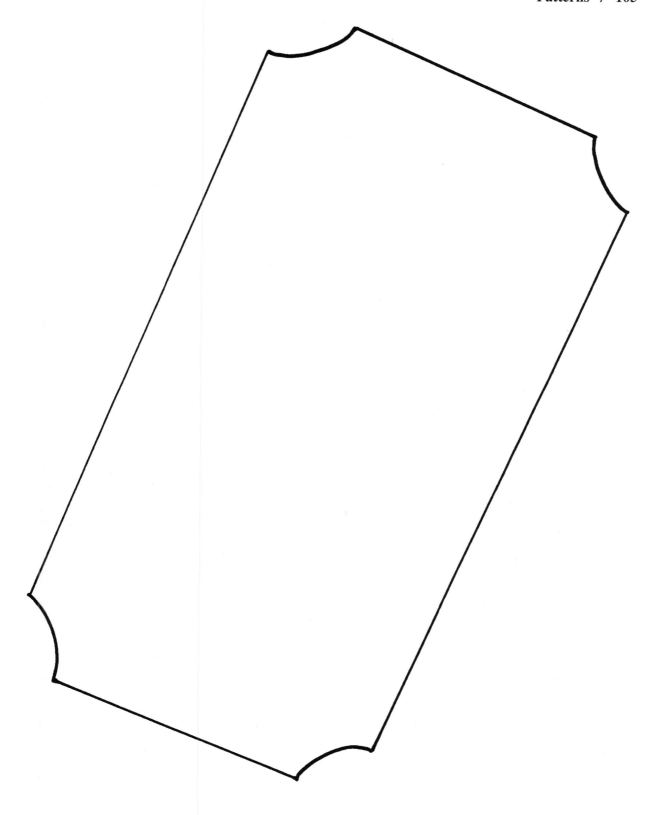

Pattern 30

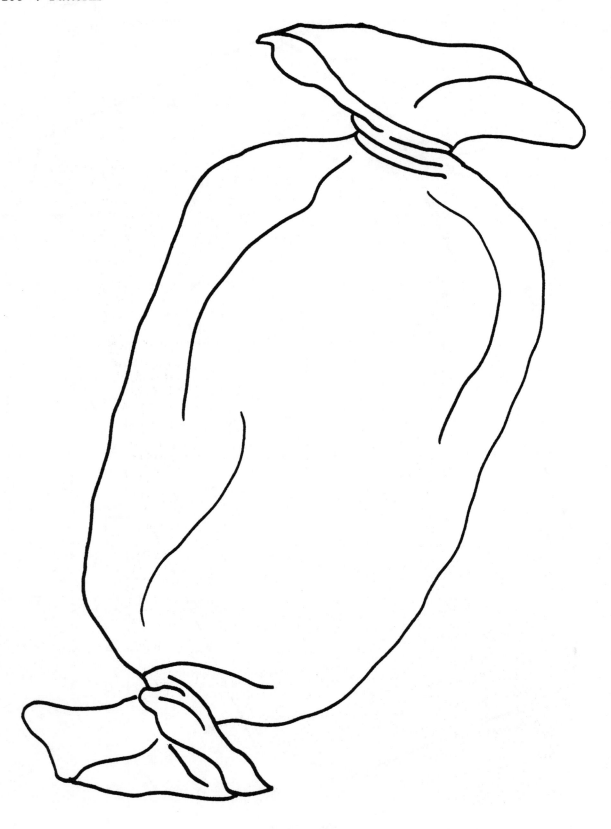

Pattern 31

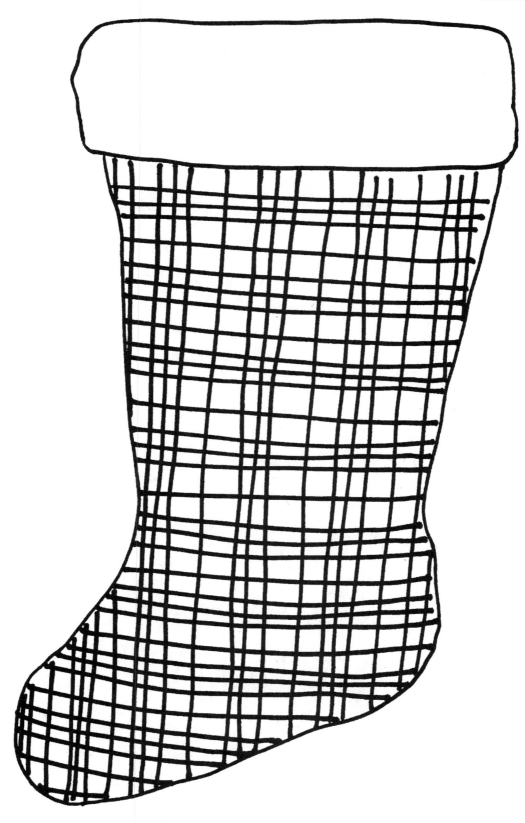

Pattern 32

Pattern 33

Pattern 34

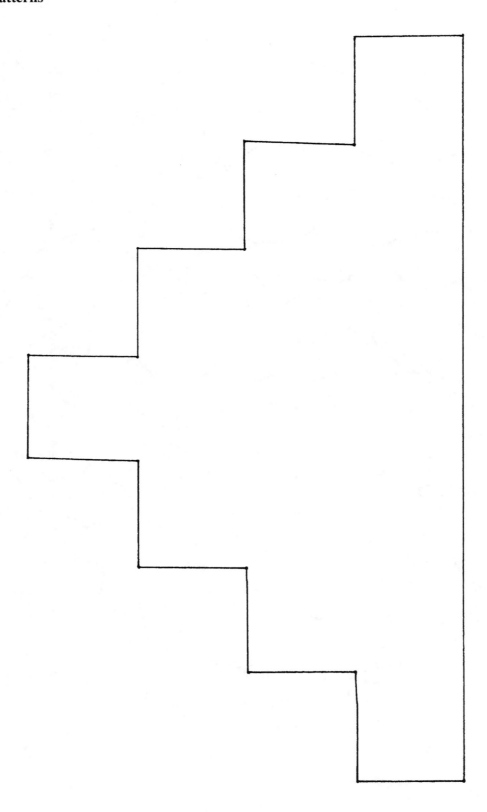

Pattern 35

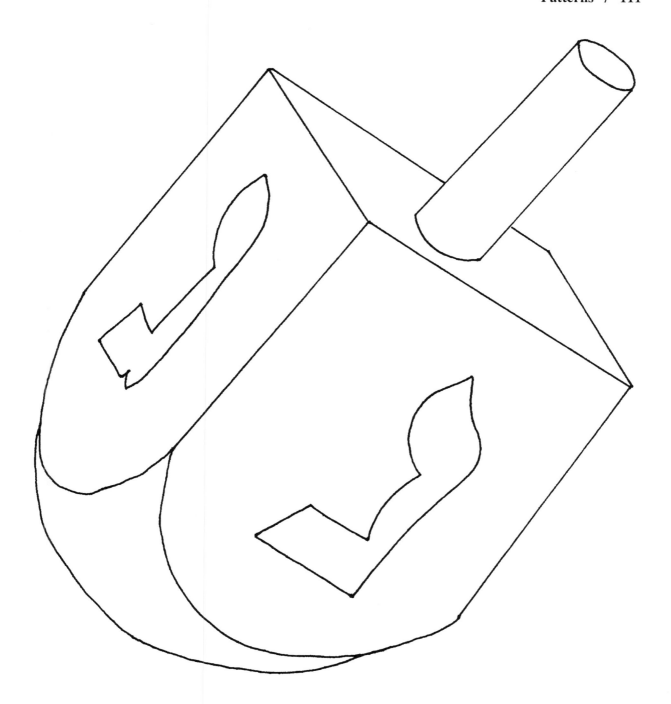

Pattern 36

Index